796.077 Mur
urray, Julie
oaches

$27.07
on1050870731

3 4028 09496 8345
HARRIS COUNTY PUBLIC LIBRARY

W9-AUU-884

Coaches

Julie Murray

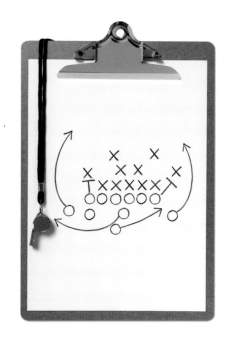

Abdo Kids Junior
is an Imprint of Abdo Kids
abdopublishing.com

Abdo
MY COMMUNITY: JOBS
Kids

abdopublishing.com

Published by Abdo Kids, a division of ABDO, P.O. Box 398166, Minneapolis, Minnesota 55439.
Copyright © 2019 by Abdo Consulting Group, Inc. International copyrights reserved in all countries.
No part of this book may be reproduced in any form without written permission from the publisher.
Abdo Kids Junior™ is a trademark and logo of Abdo Kids.

Printed in the United States of America, North Mankato, Minnesota.

052018

092018

 THIS BOOK CONTAINS
RECYCLED MATERIALS

Photo Credits: Alamy, AP Images, iStock, Shutterstock

Production Contributors: Teddy Borth, Jennie Forsberg, Grace Hansen

Design Contributors: Christina Doffing, Candice Keimig, Dorothy Toth

Library of Congress Control Number: 2017960552
Publisher's Cataloging-in-Publication Data

Names: Murray, Julie, author.

Title: Coaches / by Julie Murray.

Description: Minneapolis, Minnesota : Abdo Kids, 2019. | Series: My community: Jobs |
    Includes glossary, index and online resources (page 24).

Identifiers: ISBN 9781532107870 (lib.bdg.) | ISBN 9781532108853 (ebook) |
    ISBN 9781532109348 (Read-to-me ebook)

Subjects: LCSH: Coaches (Athletics)--Juvenile literature. | Occupations--Careers--Jobs--Juvenile
    literature. | Community life--Juvenile literature.

Classification: DDC 796.077--dc23

Table of Contents

Coaches 4

A Coach's Tools 22

Glossary 23

Index 24

Abdo Kids Code 24

Coaches

Cara is a coach. She loves her job!

Coaches help others. Bill helps
Sam hit the ball.

They set up practices. Andy works on his free throw.

9

They run drills. Leah kicks
the ball.

They help with skills. Paul

shows how to tackle.

13

They teach **teamwork**.

They help at games. Dan shows the next play.

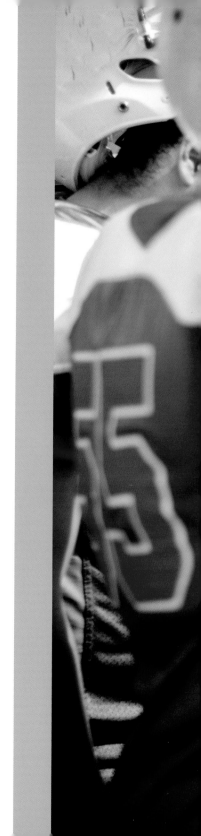

They cheer on their team.

Ana's dad coaches her team.

They won the game!

A Coach's Tools

clipboard

equipment

team

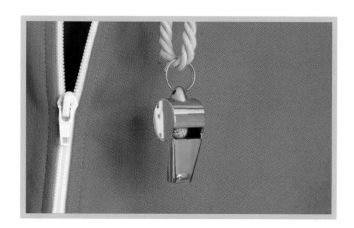

whistle

Glossary

drill

a training method in which an action is repeated over and over.

teamwork

the working together of a group of people.

skill

a certain ability.

Index

cheer 18

drill 10

game 16, 20

help 6, 12, 16

play 16

practice 8

skills 6, 8, 10, 12

teach 14

teamwork 14

Abdo Kids
ONLINE
FREE! ONLINE MULTIMEDIA RESOURCES

Visit **abdokids.com** and use this code to access crafts, games, videos, and more!

Abdo Kids Code:
MCK7870

HARRIS COUNTY PUBLIC LIBRARY
HOUSTON. TEXAS